"Feel Better—Look Better—Now!"

Introduction by Roger Duhamel,
Queen's Printer

When the Royal Canadian Air Force went about setting up a physical fitness program in the years following World War II, it based its plans on three basic facts:

- physical fitness is a direct result of physical activity;

- physical activity leading to physical fitness must be vigorous and regular;

- people will accept challenge.

After two years of painstaking research, an RCAF team of doctors, scientists, physical education specialists and artists produced the 5BX and XBX Plans for Physical Fitness. These five basic exercises for men and ten basic exercises for women were designed to provide everyone, no matter what age or physical condition, with the opportunity to achieve and maintain desirable levels of physical fitness. And it only required a very small portion of the day—11 minutes for men, 12 minutes for women.

The result has made both fitness and publishing history. Although there have been innumerable works written on the subject, never was one received with such enthusiasm as the two series of exercises offered in this book. When the Office of the Queen's Printer made them available to the public, the booklets grew into all-time Canadian best sellers. At first a few thousand, soon over a hundred thousand, now over a million Canadians have taken to the 5BX and XBX Plans. Praised by medical authorities, endorsed by Physical Fitness Organizations, the exercises have become a daily habit in most Canadian homes.

Reports that the RCAF had designed a unique, simple way to keep fit quickly spread abroad. Requests for information began to pour into Canadà from many countries. In the United States, THIS WEEK MAGAZINE reported on the publishing phenomenon

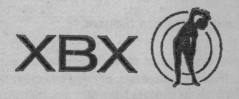

XBX

12-MINUTE-A-DAY
PLAN FOR WOMEN

and arranged to offer the exercises to its 14 million families.

In a year, half a million copies were sold by mail, and now Simon & Schuster, Inc. is also offering the exercises to the American public through bookstores. This edition follows exactly the Royal Canadian Air Force edition; not a word has been changed.

The RCAF way to keep fit is now yours for only a few minutes of your time each day. Read the instructions carefully, start at the bottom of Chart One, and away you go on the road to FEELING BETTER and LOOK-ING BETTER!

Roger Duhamel
Queen's Printer
Ottawa, Canada

5BX

11-MINUTE-A-DAY
PLAN FOR MEN

Royal Canadian Air Force
Exercise Plans for Physical Fitness
was originally published by
Information Canada.

Royal Canadian Air Force Exercise Plans for Physical Fitness

PUBLISHED BY POCKET BOOKS NEW YORK

ROYAL CANADIAN AIR FORCE EXERCISE PLANS
FOR PHYSICAL FITNESS

Revised RCAF edition published 1962

ESSANDESS SPECIAL edition published December, 1962

POCKET BOOK edition published May, 1972
9th printing .... March, 1976

This POCKET BOOK edition includes every word contained in
the original, higher-priced edition. It is printed from brand-
new plates made from completely reset, clear, easy-to-read type.
POCKET BOOK editions are published by
POCKET BOOKS,
a division of Simon & Schuster, Inc.,
A GULF+WESTERN COMPANY
630 Fifth Avenue,
New York, N.Y. 10020.
Trademarks registered in the United States
and other countries.

Standard Book Number: 0-671-80592-4.
This POCKET BOOK edition is published by arrangement
with Information Canada. Crown copyright, ©, 1962, Ottawa,
Canada: All rights reserved.

Printed in Canada.

ACKNOWLEDGMENT

The RCAF acknowledges the contributions made to the preparation of this book by physical education experts, RCAF medical advisers and P. J. Carey, D.A., Art and Craft Specialist. In addition, the RCAF particularly acknowledges the contribution of W. A. R. Orban, PhD, to the 5BX Section and of N. J. Ashton, BSc, MS, Physical Education Specialist to the XBX Section.

The kind permission of the Royal Canadian Air Force to make the text of this training book available to the public is gratefully acknowledged.

Published in the United States by Simon & Schuster, Inc. by special arrangement with Information Canada.

Contents

The
XBX
Plan
FOR WOMEN

---

10 Tested Exercises

12 Minutes a Day

The Official RCAF Fitness Plan

CAUTION

Before you start

If you have any doubt as to your capability to undertake this program, see your <u>medical</u> adviser.

You should not perform fast, vigorous, or highly competitive physical activity without gradually developing, and continuously maintaining, an adequate level of physical fitness, particularly if you are over the age of 30.

Physical Fitness—What It Means

The question is frequently asked, "What is meant by physical fitness?" Technically, physical fitness involves measures and levels of muscular strength and endurance, muscle tone, heart action and response to activity, agility, balance, co-ordination, and so on. But fitness is also a personal thing. It is how we feel when we get up in the morning; how tired or fresh we are after a hard day's work; how eagerly we look forward to doing those things which we all like to do—picnic, ski—or those things which we have to do—wash floors.

Each person is her own best judge of what physical fitness is and what it means to her.

Why You Should Be Fit

Research has shown that:

the physically fit person is able to withstand fatigue for longer periods than the unfit;

the physically fit person is better equipped to tolerate physical stress;

the physically fit person has a stronger and more efficient heart; and

there is a relationship between good mental alertness, absence of nervous tension, and physical fitness.

Remember that:

weak stomach muscles cause sagging abdomens; and weak back muscles are a major cause of back pain.

There are countless reasons for being fit. YOU know how you feel. EVERYONE knows how you look. Regular exercise can improve YOUR sense of well-being and your appearance.

Fitness is necessary for the fullest enjoyment of living.

Read the XBX booklet carefully.

Your Appearance

Your appearance is controlled by the bony frame of your body, and by the proportions of fat and muscle which you have added to it. You cannot do anything about your skeleton, but you can, and should, do something about the fat and muscle.

All of us require a certain amount of fat on and in our bodies for functional reasons. Fat softens the bony contours of the body; it helps to keep the body temperature constant; and it acts as an energy storage

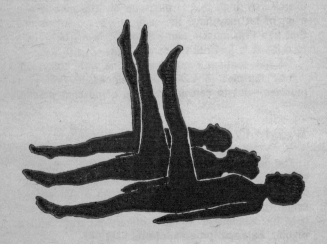

vault. Fat appears in layers on the outside of the body, covers and lines the internal organs—the heart and blood vessels, for example—and it also makes up a part of muscle.

Except for certain neurotic or glandular conditions, people are over FAT because they over EAT and under EXERCISE.

Muscle is the other controllable factor in the appearance. When we are young we are fairly active; the muscles of our bodies are used and they retain that pleasing firmness—MUSCLE TONE. The less we exercise muscles the softer and more flabby they become. They become small with disuse, less elastic, and much weaker. Much of what is considered fatness in the abdominal region is nothing more than weak stomach muscles which permit the internal organs to sag forward. Your muscles perform the same function as a girdle—keep them as resilient as your foundation garment.

Because the condition of your muscles is so important to the way you look and feel, diet alone is not the best method for trying to improve your body measurements. The best method is a combination of diet and exercise. A thigh that is made up of little muscle and a lot of fat may have the same measurement as one that has firm muscle and a light fat layer, but—let's face it—it is just not the same thigh.

Do not confuse good muscle tone with bulky, unsightly muscles. The XBX is designed to firm your muscles—not to convert you into a muscled woman.

Weight Control

The major purpose of weight control is to reduce the amount of fat on the body and to increase the amount of muscle. It is, in reality, a program of fat control rather than weight control. This control can be exerted only by coupling a sensible dietary program with a regular, balanced program of exercise.

When we eat, the food is used, stored, or discarded. The body stores fuel, or calories, as fat. The more fuel we consume, and the less of it we use, then the more of it that is stored in the body in the form of fat. The human body is not like a car's gas tank that will overflow when full. Our bodies accept all the calories that we put into them, and store those which we do not use.

For example, if you eat food that has a value of 3,000 calories and use only 2,600 of them in your activity, then the remaining 400 calories are stored in

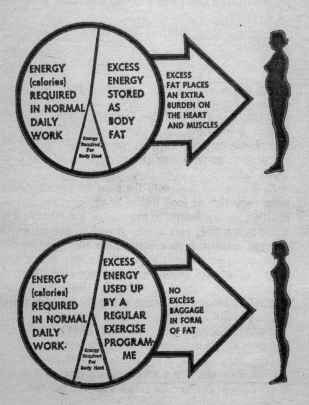

ENERGY (calories) REQUIRED IN NORMAL DAILY WORK

Energy Required For Body Heat

EXCESS ENERGY STORED AS BODY FAT

EXCESS FAT PLACES AN EXTRA BURDEN ON THE HEART AND MUSCLES

ENERGY (calories) REQUIRED IN NORMAL DAILY WORK.

Energy Required For Body Heat

EXCESS ENERGY USED UP BY A REGULAR EXERCISE PROGRAM-ME

NO EXCESS BAGGAGE IN FORM OF FAT

the body. Every time you accumulate about 4,000 of these calories you will notice an extra pound of weight on the scales.

When you exercise you burn calories. Energy used in this way will result in muscle development. As muscle is slightly heavier than fat, you may very well notice an increase in your weight rather than a reduction. However it must be stressed that this muscle weight is useful weight and will improve the way you look and feel.

Research has shown clearly that the most effective way of taking off weight and keeping it off is through a program which combines exercise and diet.

Diet

For many women, the knowledge that they have gained a few pounds, or added a few inches, causes what may be called the "Diet Reflex". Without pause to consult a medical expert they resort immediately to their favourite diet, which is more usually a fast. If you wish to go on a stringent diet—consult your physician first.

As a rule you can avoid the need for resorting to a strict reduction of food intake by the constant use of sensible dietary habits. In the normal individual, fat is added to the body very slowly. It may be several weeks or even months before you notice this gradual accumulation. You cannot hope to take this fat off and keep it off without making subtle changes in eating and exercise habits. After a "crash diet", you will undoubtedly return to your old habits and, once more, in a few weeks you will note that IT is back again.

A slight change in diet (along with XBX) can take off, and keep off, several pounds of excess fat over a period of time. For example, if you eat bread with your meals, eat one slice less; add a little less sugar, or none at all, to your tea or coffee. The calories so avoided each day

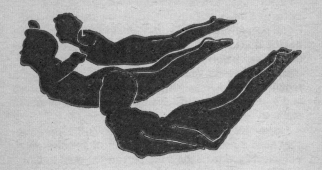

add up to several thousand in a few months and may be the difference between the way you look and feel and the way you would like to look and feel. By the time you have arrived at the condition you desire your habits will have been changed enough so that you will probably not slip back into the old ones.

What You Can Do About Fitness

Unless you are engaged in a full time program of conditioning for athletic endeavours you should take part in some form of active exercise.

The average woman is engaged in one of three activities daily—school, employment, or housework. None of these provides the balanced activity for the body that is desirable for good physical fitness. Housework, for example, though it may involve a good deal of hard physical labour, does not take into account the flexibility of the muscles, nor does it work all the muscles of the body. Day after day you do the same things. The muscles that work get plenty of exercise; the others get little or none.

The same facts that are true of housework also hold true for most sports. Sports make specific contributions to fitness but do not condition the whole body. Most people taking part in a recreation sport do not pursue it vigorously enough to develop adequate levels of fitness. Before they become completely effective, even those sports which can produce all round fitness require more skill than the average person possesses and more time than the average person can devote to them.

No matter what you do in your daily life you probably need a good, balanced program of exercise which will enable you to become the person you want to be.

How You Can Use XBX

XBX requires little time and space, and no equipment, so you can:

Do it alone—at home—at any time.

Form your own fitness club. Make XBX a part of your daily or weekly get together with "the girls".

Have your family work on fitness together. XBX for the ladies, 5BX for the men. It can be fun.

Why XBX Was Developed

Research has indicated that Canadians—male and female, young and old—are in need of some form of regular, vigorous, physical activity. As more and more labour-saving devices are put into general use, as more and more people watch more and more television, movies, and sports events, the amount of physical effort expended by the average person decreases continually.

An analysis of the exercise needs of Canadians was conducted by RCAF specialists and led to the development of the 5BX program for men. XBX is the complementary program for women.

The RCAF analysis indicated three major deterrents to regular exercise:

first —a great majority of people would like to exercise, but do not know how to go about it—what to do, how to do it, how often, how to progress, or how far to progress;

second—most exercise programs call for the use of equipment and gymnasiums which are not always available; and

third —most exercise programs call for a great expenditure of time, which most people cannot spare.

Clearly a program which resolves these problems is required.

The XBX Plan does this.

XBX tells you what to do, where to start, how fast you progress, and how far you should progress to achieve a desirable level of physical fitness.

XBX requires no equipment and very little space.

XBX takes only 12 minutes a day.

The program is here—the rest is up to you.

How XBX Was Developed

XBX is the product of extensive research into the problems of physical fitness for girls and women.

The research was conducted at several RCAF stations and in the later stages included sections of the civilian population.

Over 600 girls and women of all ages participated in the project. The RCAF is indebted to these persons for their contributions to the program.

The first step in the project was the administration of a series of physical fitness tests. The tests included an examination of muscular strength and endurance, testing of heart response to activity, and measurement of fat layers. From the results of these tests the physical fitness needs of women were analyzed.

Experiments were carried out with a wide variety of exercises to determine those most effective in producing the desired results. Many of these exercises were discarded as ineffectual. The ten exercises of XBX provided the most balanced and effective program.

The time limits for each exercise were varied until the optimum time for good results was determined.

Tests were conducted to arrive at the number of times each exercise could be done, and should be done, within the time limits.

The first experimental exercise programs were used by several hundred women. Periodic tests showed that XBX was an effective plan to improve levels of general fitness.

The program was then distributed to groups and to individuals across Canada for further trial and comment. Further modifications in the plan were made on the basis of this final field trial.

The results of this research are presented in this booklet—RCAF XBX Plan for Physical Fitness.

What the XBX Plan Is

The XBX Plan is a physical fitness program composed of four charts of ten exercises, arranged in progressive order of difficulty. The ten exercises on each chart are always performed in the same order, and in the same maximum time limits.

The charts are divided into levels. There are 48 levels in all, 12 in each chart. The levels are numbered consecutively, starting with 1 at the bottom of Chart I and ending with 48 at the top of Chart IV.

In addition to the regular exercises, two supplementary exercises are available for Charts I, II, and III. These exercises are for the muscles of the feet and ankles and for those muscles which assist in the maintenance of good posture.

How XBX Works

Any exercise plan or program should work on the basis of an easy start and gradual progression. As physical fitness improves, the work load is increased. The XBX approach to exercise follows these principles.

XBX incorporates two methods to make the work load greater:

first —the time limit for each exercise remains the same in all charts, but the number of times the exercise is performed within this time limit is increased at each level within each chart; and

second—the exercises are made more difficult from each chart to the next higher one.

On each chart you do the same exercises at each of the twelve levels but increase the number of times you do them.

As you move to the next higher chart the exercises are basically the same but have been modified and made slightly more demanding.

The XBX has been planned for gradual, painless progression.

Follow the plan as outlined in the booklet.

Do not skip levels.

Do not progress faster than is recommended.

What the Exercises Are For

The XBX will improve your general physical condition by:

increasing muscle tone;

increasing muscular strength;

increasing muscular endurance;

increasing flexibility; and

increasing the efficiency of your heart.

Each exercise is included because of its contribution in one or more of these areas.

The first four exercises are primarily to improve and maintain flexibility and mobility in those areas of the body which are usually neglected. They also serve as a warm-up for the more strenuous exercises which follow.

Exercise 5 is for strengthening the abdominal region and the muscles of the fronts of the thighs.

Exercise 6 exercises the long muscles of the back, the buttocks, and the backs of the thighs.

Exercise 7 concentrates on the muscles on the sides of the thighs. These muscles get very little work in routine daily activities, or indeed in most sports.

Exercise 8 is primarily for the arms, shoulders, and chest, but at the same time exercises the back and abdomen.

Exercise 9 is partly for flexibility in the waist area and for strengthening the muscles of the hips and sides.

Exercise 10, the run-in-place with jumping, while exercising the legs, is primarily for the conditioning of the heart and lungs.

The two supplementary exercises are included for those who wish to do a little more. One exercise is for strengthening the muscles of the feet and the ankle joint. The other is for those muscles of the back and abdomen which assist in the maintenance of posture.

What the Charts Mean

Following is an explanation of what the chart pages mean. Check the paragraph headings with the sample chart on pages 30–31.

EXERCISE

The numbers across the tops of the charts are the exercise numbers from 1 to 10. The column headed 1 refers to Exercise 1, and so on. The exercises are described and illustrated in the ten pages following each chart. Exercises 8A and 8B are the supplementary exercises described on pages 84 to 89. If you choose to do these, do them between Exercises 8 and 9.

LEVEL

The numbers along the left side of the chart are the levels of the program, and each refers to the line of numbers beside it under the exercise headings. For example at Level 14 you do Exercise 3 seven times, Exercise 6 fifteen times, and so on.

MINUTES FOR EACH EXERCISE

The allotted time for each exercise is shown here. The exercises numbered 1 to 4 are the warm-up and all four are to be completed within 2 minutes, or about a half minute each. Other examples: Exercise 5 takes 2 minutes, and Exercise 6 takes 1 minute. The total time for each level of ten exercises is 12 minutes. It is important that all the exercises be done within this total time limit. Do not move up to the next level until you can do your present level, without excessive strain or fatigue, in the 12 minutes.

RECOMMENDED NUMBER OF DAYS AT EACH LEVEL

Record in the box provided on each chart page the number of days it is recommended that you spend at each level before progressing to the next. (See instructions for using the plan on pages 34—35.)

MY PROGRESS

This chart is provided to enable you to keep an accurate record of your progress on the way to your physical fitness goal. Record the dates you started and finished each level. Make a note of how you felt as you did the exercises. To use the bottom chart, select a reasonable aim for yourself in terms of body measurements and record this in MY AIM. Then record your present measurements on the START line. When you have completed the exercise chart, note your latest measurements on the line labelled FINISH. The FINISH line on one chart will be the START line on the next.

Note: Do not expect startling results. Fitness takes time and persistence. Couple your XBX program with a good diet, and your progress will be steady.

NOTE: This chart is for illustration only. Charts for use start on Pages 36-37.

CHART II

LEVEL	1	2	3	4	5	6	7	8	9	10	8A	8B
24	15	16	12	30	35	38	50	28	20	210	40	36
23	15	16	12	30	33	36	48	26	18	200	38	34
22	15	16	12	30	31	34	46	24	18	200	36	32
21	13	14	11	26	29	32	44	23	16	190	33	29
20	13	14	11	26	27	31	42	21	16	175	31	27
19	13	14	11	26	24	29	40	20	14	160	28	24
18	12	12	9	20	22	27	38	18	14	150	25	22
17	12	12	9	20	19	24	36	16	12	150	22	20
16	12	12	9	20	16	21	34	14	10	140	19	19
15	10	10	7	18	14	18	32	12	10	130	17	15
14	10	10	7	18	11	15	30	10	8	120	14	13
13	10	10	7	18	9	12	28	8	8	120	12	12
Minutes for each Exercise		2		2	2	1	1	2	1	3	1	1

EXERCISE

Recommended number of days at each level

MY PROGRESS

LEVEL	STARTED	FINISHED	COMMENTS
24			
23			
22			
21			
20			
19			
18			
17			
16			
15			
14			
13			

	DATE	HEIGHT	WEIGHT	WAIST	HIPS	BUST
My Aim						
Start						
Finish						

Your Fitness Goal

As is explained in the instructions for the use of the program on the opposite page, each age group is given a physical fitness goal to attain; that is, a level which they should try to reach.

The goals indicated in this plan are based on the average achievements of girls and women who have participated in it.

Your goal, then, is the level of fitness that the average girl or woman of your age reached without undue stress, strain, or fatigue.

With every average, there are individuals who surpass it, and those who fall below it. In terms of the XBX plan and the goals, this means that there will be some women who are capable of progressing beyond the goal indicated, and on the other hand, there will be persons who will never attain this average level.

If you feel able to move further through the charts than your goal, by all means do so. If, on the contrary, you experience great difficulty in approaching this level you should stop at a level which you feel to be within your capability. It is impossible to predict accurately a level for each individual who uses this program. Use the goals as guides, and apply them with common sense.

From time to time as you progress through the levels you may have difficulty with a particular level or exercise. If so, proceed slowly but keep working at it. (These "plateaus" may occur anywhere in the progression.) Generally you will be able to move ahead after a few days at this level. If you cannot, then you have probably arrived at your potential physical fitness level in so far as this particular program is concerned.

Caution

If for any reason you stop doing XBX for more than two weeks because of illness, vacation, or any other cause—DO NOT restart at the level you had attained before stopping. DO drop back several levels or to the next lower chart until you find a level which you can do fairly easily. Physical fitness is lost during long periods of inactivity. This is particularly true if the inactivity were caused by illness.

Instructions for Using the XBX Plan

First select YOUR GOAL for YOUR AGE from the table below. Locate this level in the charts which follow. Mark it in some way—circle it or underline it.

Record the recommended minimum number of days at each level in the box provided on each chart page. For example if you are 28 years of age, your goal is Level 30 on Chart III and you spend AT LEAST 2 days doing each level on Chart I, 3 days at each level on Chart II, and 5 days at each level on Chart III. Do not move faster than the recommended rate.

If Your Age is	Your Goal is Level	Recommended Minimum Number of Days at Each Level on			
		Chart I	Chart II	Chart III	Chart IV
7- 8 years	30	1	1	2	x
9-10 years	34	1	1	2	x
11-12 years	38	1	1	2	3
13-14 years	41	1	1	2	3
15-17 years	44	1	1	2	3
18-19 years	40	1	2	3	4
20-25 years	35	1	2	3	x
26-30 years	30	2	3	5	x
31-35 years	26	2	4	6	x
36-40 years	22	4	6	x	x
41-45 years	19	5	7	x	x
46-50 years	16	7	8	x	x
51-55 years	11	8	x	x	x

To Start and Progress

Start at Level 1, which is at the bottom of Chart I. When you can do this level without strain and in 12 minutes move up to Level 2. Continue through the levels and charts in this way until you reach the goal level recommended for your age group, OR until you feel you are exercising at your maximum capacity.

When You Reach Your Goal

Once you have reached your goal you should require only three exercise periods a week to maintain it.

CHART I

LEVEL	EXERCISE											
	1	2	3	4	5	6	7	8	9	10	8A	8B
12	9	8	10	40	26	20	28	14	14	170	18	20
11	9	8	10	40	24	18	26	13	14	160	17	18
10	9	8	10	40	22	16	25	12	12	150	16	17
9	7	7	8	36	20	14	23	10	11	140	14	15
8	7	7	8	36	18	12	20	9	10	125	13	14
7	7	7	8	36	16	12	18	8	10	115	11	12
6	5	5	7	28	14	10	16	7	8	100	10	11
5	5	5	7	28	12	8	13	6	6	90	8	9
4	5	5	7	28	10	8	10	5	6	80	7	8
3	3	4	5	24	8	6	8	4	4	70	6	6
2	3	4	5	24	6	4	6	3	3	60	5	5
1	3	4	5	24	4	4	4	3	2	50	4	3
Minutes for each Exercise		2			2	1	1	2	1	3	1	1

Recommended number of days at each level

MY PROGRESS

LEVEL	STARTED	FINISHED	COMMENTS
12			
11			
10			
9			
8			
7			
6			
5			
4			
3			
2			
1			

	DATE	HEIGHT	WEIGHT	WAIST	HIPS	BUST
My Aim						
Start						
Finish						

Exercise 1—Toe Touching

Start. Stand erect, feet 12 inches apart, arms over head.

Bend forward to touch floor between feet. Do not try to keep knees straight. Return to starting position.

Count. Each return to starting position counts one.

Exercise 2—Knee Raising

Start. Stand erect, hands at sides, feet together.

Raise left knee as high as possible, grasping knee and shin with hands.

Pull leg toward body. Keep back straight throughout. Lower foot to floor.

Repeat with right leg. Continue by alternating legs—left then right.

Count. Left and right knee raises count one.

Exercise 3—Lateral Bending

Start. Stand erect, feet 12 inches apart, hands at sides. Keeping back straight, bend sidewards from waist to left. Slide left hand down leg as far as possible. Return to starting position and bend to right side. Continue by alternating to left then right.

Count. Bends to the left and right count one.

Exercise 4—Arm Circling

Start. Stand erect, feet 12 inches apart, arms at sides. Make large circles with left arm. Do one quarter of total count with forward circles and one quarter with backward circles. Repeat with right arm.

Count. A full arm circle counts one.

Exercise 5—Partial Sit-ups

Start. Lie on back, legs straight and together, arms at sides.

Raise head and shoulders from floor until you can see your heels. Lower head to floor.

Count. Each partial sit-up counts one.

Exercise 6—Chest and Leg Raising

Start. Lie face down, arms along sides, hands under thighs, palms pressing against thighs.

Raise head, shoulders, and left leg as high as possible from floor. Keep leg straight. Lower to floor.

Repeat raising head, shoulders, and right leg.

Continue by alternating legs, left then right.

Count. Each chest and leg raise counts one.

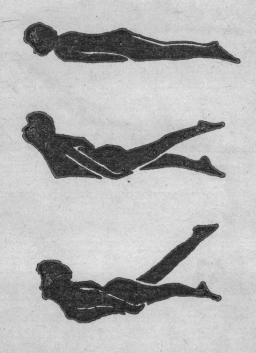

Exercise 7—Side Leg Raising

Start. Lie on side, legs straight, lower arm stretched over head along floor, top arm used for balance.

Raise upper leg 18 to 24 inches. Lower to starting position.

Count. Each leg raise counts one. Do half number of counts raising left leg. Roll to other side and do half number of counts raising right leg.

Exercise 8—Push-ups

Start. Lie face down, legs straight and together, hands directly under shoulders.

Push body off floor in any way possible, keeping hands and knees in contact with floor. Sit back on heels. Lower body to floor.

Count. Each return to starting position counts one.

Exercise 9—Leg Lifting

Start. Lie on back, legs straight and together, arms at sides, palms down.

Raise left leg until it is perpendicular to floor, or as close to this position as possible.

Lower and repeat with right leg.

Continue by alternating legs, left then right.

Count. Left plus right leg lifts count one.

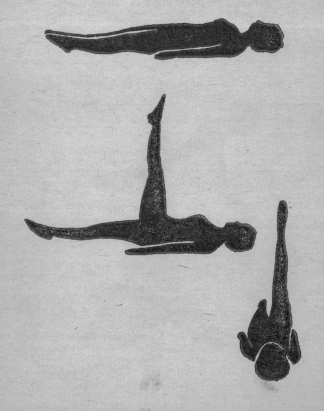

Exercise 10—Run and Hop

Start. Stand erect, feet together, arms at sides.

Starting with left leg, run in place raising feet at least four inches from floor.

(When running in place lift knees forward, do not merely kick heels backwards.)

Count. Each time left foot touches floor counts one.

After each fifty counts do ten hops.

Hops. Hopping is done so that both feet leave floor together. Try to hop at least four inches off floor each time.

Note: In all run-in-place exercises only running steps are counted towards completing exercise repetitions.

CHART II

			EXERCISE										
	1	**2**	**3**	**4**	**5**	**6**	**7**	**8**	**9**	**10**	**8A**	**8B**
L 24	15	16	12	30	35	38	50	28	20	210	40	36
23	15	16	12	30	33	36	48	26	18	200	38	34
22	15	16	12	30	31	34	46	24	18	200	36	32
E 21	13	14	11	26	29	32	44	23	16	190	33	29
20	13	14	11	26	27	31	42	21	16	175	31	27
V 19	13	14	11	26	24	29	40	20	14	160	28	24
18	12	12	9	20	22	27	38	18	14	150	25	22
E 17	12	12	9	20	19	24	36	16	12	150	22	20
16	12	12	9	20	16	21	34	14	10	140	19	19
L 15	10	10	7	18	14	18	32	12	10	130	17	15
14	10	10	7	18	11	15	30	10	8	120	14	13
13	10	10	7	18	9	12	28	8	8	120	12	12
Minutes for each Exercise			2		2	1	1	2	1	3	1	1

Recommended number of days at each level

48

MY PROGRESS

LEVEL	STARTED	FINISHED	COMMENTS
24			
23			
22			
21			
20			
19			
18			
17			
16			
15			
14			
13			

	DATE	HEIGHT	WEIGHT	WAIST	HIPS	BUST
My Aim						
Start						
Finish						

Exercise 1—Toe Touching

Start. Stand erect, feet 12 inches apart, arms over head.

Bend forward to touch floor between feet.

Bob up and down touching floor a second time.

Return to starting position.

Count. Each return to starting position counts one.

Exercise 2—Knee Raising

Start. Stand erect, feet together, arms at sides.

Raise left knee as high as possible grasping knee and shin with hands.

Pull leg against body. Keep back straight throughout. Lower foot to floor.

Repeat with right leg. Continue by alternating legs—left then right.

Count. Left and right knee raises count one.

Exercise 3—Lateral Bending

Start. Stand erect, feet 12 inches apart, hands at sides.

Keeping back straight, bend sidewards from waist to left. Slide left hand down leg as far as possible.

Bob up a few inches and press sidewards and down again.

Return to starting position and repeat same movements to right side.

Continue by alternating to left then right.

Count. Bends to left and right count one.

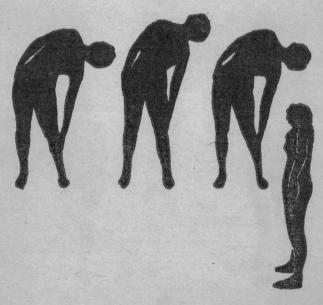

Exercise 4—Arm Circling

Start. Stand erect, feet 12 inches apart, arms at sides.

Make large circles, with both arms at same time, backwards and around. Do half the number of repetitions making backward circles and half making forward circles.

Count. Each full arm circle counts one.

Exercise 5—Rocking Sit-ups

Start. Lie on back, knees bent, feet on floor, arms extended over head.

Swing arms forward and at same time thrust feet forward and move to sitting position. Reach forward, trying to touch toes with fingers. Return to starting position.

Count. Each return to starting position counts one.

Exercise 6—Chest and Leg Raising

Start. Lie face down, arms along sides, palms pressing against thighs.

Raise head, shoulders, and legs as high as possible from floor.

Keep legs straight. Return to starting position.

Count. Each return to starting position counts one.

Exercise 7—Side Leg Raising

Start. Lie on side, legs straight, lower arm stretched over head along floor, top arm used for balance.

Raise upper leg until it is perpendicular to floor or as close to this position as possible. Lower to starting position.

Count. Each leg raise counts one. Do half number of counts raising left leg. Roll to other side and do half number of counts raising right leg.

Exercise 8—Knee Push-ups

Start. Lie face down, legs straight and together, hands directly under shoulders.

Push body off floor until arms are straightened.

Keep hands and knees in contact with floor. Try to keep body in straight line.

Count. Each return to starting position counts one.

Exercise 9—Leg-overs

Start. Lie on back, legs straight and together, arms stretched sidewards at shoulder level.

Raise left leg to perpendicular. Drop it across body, and try to touch right hand with toes.

Raise leg to perpendicular and return to starting position. Repeat same movements with right leg. Keep body and legs straight throughout, and shoulders on floor.

Count. Each return to starting position counts one.

Exercise 10—Run and Stride Jumping

Start. Stand erect, feet together, arms at sides. Starting with left leg run in place raising feet at least four inches from floor.

Count. Each time left foot touches floor counts one.

After each fifty runs do ten stride jumps.

Stride Jump. Stride jump starts with feet together, arms at sides. Jump so that feet are about 18 inches apart when you land. At the same time as you jump, raise arms sidewards to shoulder height. Jump again so that feet are together and arms are at sides when you land.

CHART III

	EXERCISE											
	1	2	3	4	5	6	7	8	9	10	8A	8B
36	15	22	18	40	42	40	60	40	20	240	32	38
L 35	15	22	18	40	41	39	60	39	20	230	30	36
34	15	22	18	40	40	38	58	37	19	220	29	34
E 33	13	20	16	36	39	36	58	35	19	210	27	33
32	13	20	16	36	37	36	56	34	18	200	25	31
V 31	13	20	16	36	35	34	56	32	16	200	24	30
30	12	18	14	30	33	33	54	30	15	190	23	28
E 29	12	18	14	30	32	31	54	29	14	180	21	26
28	12	18	14	30	31	30	52	27	12	170	20	25
L 27	10	16	12	24	29	30	52	25	11	160	19	23
26	10	16	12	24	27	29	50	23	9	150	17	21
25	10	16	12	24	26	28	48	22	8	140	16	20
Minutes for each Exercise			2									
Recommended number of days at each level	1	2			2	1	1	2	1	3	1	1

MY PROGRESS

LEVEL	STARTED	FINISHED	COMMENTS
36			
35			
34			
33			
32			
31			
30			
29			
28			
27			
26			
25			

	DATE	HEIGHT	WEIGHT	WAIST	HIPS	BUST
My Aim						
Start						
Finish						

Exercise 1—Toe Touching

Start. Stand erect, feet about 16 inches apart, arms over head.

Bend down to touch floor outside left foot. Bob up and down to touch floor between feet. Bob again and bend to touch floor outside right foot. Return to starting position.

Count. Each return to starting position counts one.

Exercise 2—Knee Raising

Start. Stand erect, feet together, arms at sides.

Raise left knee as high as possible, grasping knee and shin with hands.

Pull leg against body. Keep back straight throughout. Lower foot to floor.

Repeat with right leg. Continue by alternating legs—left then right.

Count. Left and right knee raises count one.

Exercise 3—Lateral Bending

Start. Stand erect, feet 12 inches apart, right arm extended over head, bent at elbow.

Keeping back straight, bend sidewards from waist to left.

Slide left hand down leg as far as possible, at the same time press to left with right arm.

Return to starting position and change arm positions. Repeat to right. Continue by alternating to left then right.

Count. Bends to left and right count one.

Exercise 4—Arm Circling

Start. Stand erect, feet 12 inches apart, arms at sides.

Make large circles with arms in a windmill action—one arm following other and both moving at same time.

Do half number of repetitions making backward circles and half making forward circles.

Count. Each full circle by both arms counts one.

Exercise 5—Sit-ups

Start. Lie on back, legs straight and together, arms along sides.

Keeping back as straight as possible, move to a sitting position.

Slide hands along legs during this movement finally reaching forward to try to touch toes with fingers.

Return to starting position.

Count. Each return to starting position counts one.

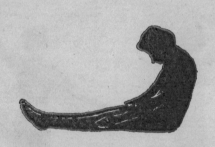

Exercise 6—Chest and Leg Raising

Start. Lie face down, legs straight and together, arms stretched sidewards at shoulder level.

Raise entire upper body and both legs from floor as high as possible.

Keep legs straight. Return to starting position.

Count. Each return to starting position counts one.

Exercise 7—Side Leg Raising

Start. Lie on side, legs straight, lower arm stretched over head along floor, top arm used for balance.

Raise upper leg until it is perpendicular to floor. Lower to starting position.

Count. Each leg raise counts one. Do half number of counts raising left leg. Roll to other side and do half number of counts raising right leg.

Exercise 8—Elbow Push-ups

Start. Lie face down, legs straight and together, elbows directly under shoulders, forearms along floor, and hands clasped together.

Raise body from floor by straightening it from head to heels.

In the up position, body is in a straight line and elbows, forearms, and toes are in contact with floor. Lower to starting position. Keep head up throughout.

Count. Each return to starting position counts one.

Exercise 9—Leg-overs—Tuck

Start. Lie on back, legs straight and together, arms stretched sidewards at shoulder level, palms down.

Raise both legs from floor, bending at hips and knees until in a tuck position. Lower legs to left, keeping knees together and both shoulders on floor. Raise legs and lower to floor on right side. Raise until perpendicular to floor and return to starting position. Keep knees close to abdomen throughout.

Count. Each return to starting position counts one.

Exercise 10—Run and Half Knee Bends

Start. Stand erect, feet together, arms at sides.

Starting with left leg, run in place raising feet at least six inches from floor.

Count. Each time left foot touches floor counts one.

After each fifty counts do ten half knee bends.

Half Knee Bends. Half knee bends start with hands on hips, feet together, body erect. Bend at knees and hips, lowering body until thigh and calf form an angle of about 110 degrees. Do not bend knees past a right angle. Keep back straight. Return to starting position.

CHART IV

	EXERCISE									
	1	2	3	4	5	6	7	8	9	10
48	15	26	15	32	48	46	58	30	16	230
L 47	15	26	15	32	45	45	56	27	15	220
46	15	26	15	32	44	44	54	24	14	210
E 45	13	24	14	30	42	43	52	21	13	200
44	13	24	14	30	40	42	50	19	13	190
V 43	13	24	14	30	38	40	48	16	12	175
42	12	22	12	28	35	39	46	13	10	160
E 41	12	22	12	28	32	38	44	11	9	150
40	12	22	12	28	30	38	40	9	8	140
L 39	10	20	10	26	29	36	38	8	7	130
38	10	20	10	26	27	35	36	7	6	115
37	10	20	10	26	25	34	34	6	5	100
Minutes for each Exercise	2			2	2	1	1	2	1	3

Recommended number of days at each level

72

MY PROGRESS

LEVEL	STARTED	FINISHED	COMMENTS
48			
47			
46			
45			
44			
43			
42			
41			
40			
39			
38			
37			

	DATE	HEIGHT	WEIGHT	WAIST	HIPS	BUST
My Aim						
Start						
Finish						

Exercise 1—Toe Touching

Start. Stand erect, feet about 16 inches apart, arms over head.

Bend down to touch floor outside left foot. Bob up and down to touch floor between feet. Bob again touching floor between feet once more. Bob and bend to touch floor outside right foot.

Return to starting position.

Count. Each return to starting position counts one.

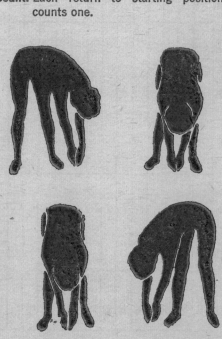

Exercise 2—Knee Raising

Start. Stand erect, feet together, arms at sides.

Raise left knee as high as possible, grasping knee and shin with hands.

Pull leg against body. Keep back straight throughout.

Lower foot to floor.

Repeat with right leg. Continue by alternating legs—left then right.

Count. Left and right knee raises count one.

Exercise 3—Lateral Bending

Start. Stand erect, feet 12 inches apart, right arm extended over head, bent at elbow.

Keeping back straight, bend sidewards from waist to left. Slide left hand down leg as far as possible, at same time press to left with right arm. Bob up a few inches and press to left again.

Return to starting position and change arm positions.

Repeat to right.

Continue by alternating to left then right.

Count. Bends to left and right count one.

Exercise 4—Arm Flinging

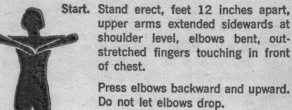

Start. Stand erect, feet 12 inches apart, upper arms extended sidewards at shoulder level, elbows bent, outstretched fingers touching in front of chest.

Press elbows backward and upward. Do not let elbows drop.

Return arms to starting position and then fling hands and arms outward, backward, and upward as far as possible.

Return to starting position.

Count. Count one after each arm fling.

Exercise 5—Sit-ups

Start. Lie on back, legs straight and together, hands behind head.

Move to sitting position. Keep feet on floor (support may be used if necessary) and back straight. Lower body to starting position.

Count. Each return to starting position counts one.

Exercise 6—Chest and Leg Raising

Start. Lie face down, legs straight and together, hands behind head.

Raise entire upper body and both legs from floor as high as possible. Keep legs straight.

Return to starting position.

Count. Each return to starting position counts one.

Exercise 7—Side Leg Raising

Start. With right side to floor, support weight on right hand (arm straight) and side of right foot, using left hand for assistance in balance if necessary.

Raise left leg until it is parallel with floor. Lower leg to starting position.

Count. Each leg raise counts one. Do half number of counts raising left leg. Change to other side and do half number of counts raising right leg.

Exercise 8—Push-ups

Start. Lie face down, legs straight and together, toes turned under, hands directly under shoulders.

Push up from hands and toes until arms are fully extended.

Keep body and legs in a straight line. Return to touch chest to floor and repeat.

Count. Each time chest touches floor counts one.

Exercise 9—Leg-overs—Straight

Start. Lie on back, legs straight and together, arms stretched sidewards at shoulder level, palms down.

Raise both legs until they are perpendicular to floor, keeping them straight and together. Lower legs to left, trying to touch left hand with toes. Raise to perpendicular and lower to right side. Raise again to perpendicular and return to starting position.

Count. Each return to starting position counts one.

Exercise 10—Run and Semi-Squat Jumps

Start. Stand erect, feet together, arms at sides.

Starting with left leg, run in place raising feet at least six inches from floor.

Count. Each time left foot touches floor counts one.

After each fifty counts do ten semi-squat jumps.

Semi-Squat Jumps. Drop to a half crouch position with hands on knees and arms straight. Keep back as straight as possible, one foot slightly ahead of the other. Jump to upright position with body straight and feet leaving floor. Reverse position of feet before landing, return to half crouch, and repeat.

Supplementary Exercises

On this page and the following five pages the supplementary exercises for feet, ankles, and posture are illustrated and described. If you wish to do these exercises they are to be included in your regular program between Exercises 8 and 9 and are numbered 8A and 8B.

Chart I

Supplementary Exercise 8A—Feet and Ankles

Start. Sit on floor, legs straight and about six inches apart, hands behind body for support, feet relaxed.

Press toes away from body as far as possible. Bring toes towards body hooking feet as much as possible. Relax feet.

Count. Each return to relaxed state counts one.

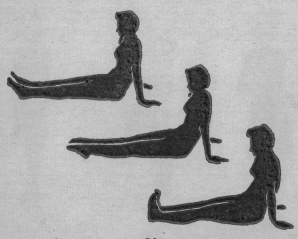

Supplementary Exercise 8B—Posture

Start. Sit on floor, knees bent, feet on floor, hands clasped about knees, head bent forward, and body relaxed.

Straighten body and lift head to look directly ahead. Pull in muscles of abdomen. Relax to starting position.

Count. Each return to starting position counts one.

Chart II

Supplementary Exercise 8A—Feet and Ankles

Start. Sit on floor, legs straight and heels about 14 inches apart, hands behind body for support, feet relaxed.

Move feet so that toes make large circular movements. Press out and around and in and towards the body. Do half number of counts moving toes in one direction, then reverse for remainder of counts.

Count. Each time toes describe a full circle counts one.

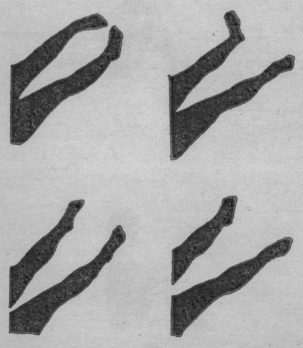

Supplementary Exercise 8B—Posture

Start. Lie on back, knees bent, feet on floor, arms slightly to side.

Relax muscles of trunk.

Press lower part of back to floor by tightening muscles of abdomen and back. Relax to starting position.

Count. Each return to starting position counts one.

Chart III

Supplementary Exercise 8A—Feet and Ankles

Start. Stand erect, arms at sides, feet about 12 inches apart.

First raise up onto toes, then lower until feet are flat on floor.

Next roll outward on sides of feet, then roll feet so that outside edge of foot is off floor. Return to starting position.

Count. Each return to starting position counts one.

Supplementary Exercise 8B—Posture

Start. Lie on back, legs straight and together, arms slightly to side.

Relax muscles of trunk.

Press lower part of back to floor by tightening muscles of abdomen and back. Relax to starting position.

Count. Each return to starting position counts one.

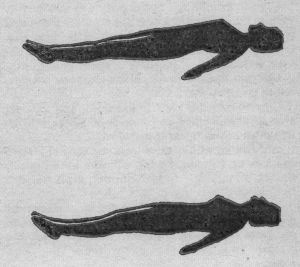

Live To Be Fit and Be Fit To Live

This pamphlet has been concerned primarily with the habits of exercise and diet as steps on the road to fitness. Many more ways and means exist which can become habits that will also contribute to this goal. Try to make some of these a part of your daily living and you will soon find that without conscious effort, or extra "work", you are gaining many benefits.

Walking is an excellent exercise if done at a faster pace than a slow shuffle. If you use public transportation do not use the nearest or most convenient stop, but get on or off a few blocks away and walk briskly. Walk to the corner store or mail box rather than using your car. At every opportunity, walk rather than ride. Climb a few flights of stairs instead of using the elevator or escalator.

Use your muscles to lift objects when you are able, rather than pushing them.

Even an everyday practice like drying yourself with a towel after bathing can become a fitness activity. Rub down briskly rather than daubing.

While sitting at a desk or table you can aid posture and tone up muscles. Sit tall with your back straight; do not slump with round back and shoulders, and head forward.

To tone up the shoulder girdle and arm muscles: sit erect, place hands on desk, palms down, elbows bent, and press down trying to lift body from chair. Hold the pressure for a few seconds. Repeat two or three times a day.

When standing, sitting, or lying, tense the muscles of the abdomen and hold for about six seconds. Do this a few times each day.

Constantly think of how you look, and walk tall and sit tall, always attempting to maintain a good postural position.

WALKING IS A "BEST" EXERCISE

Rest, Relaxation, and Revitalization

It is just as important that your body receive adequate rest as it is that it be exercised. Sleep requirements vary from person to person and each person is her own best judge of her needs. The important thing is to awake refreshed and revitalized. A few tips on getting the most from your bedtime hours:

Keep the room as dark as possible;

Do not take your problems to bed with you—if you must think, think calm, restful thoughts;

Mild exercise before retiring may be helpful;

If you are hungry, have a light snack or a warm, non-stimulating beverage.

Relaxation, both mental and physical, is becoming more and more essential in the fast moving, hurly-burly world in which we live. Many emotional tensions are reflected in physical (organic and muscular) tensions.

You can consciously reduce both forms of tension. Physically you can learn to relax muscle groups. A simple illustration is: hold your hands in front of you, tighten up the muscles of the forearms so that the hands and fingers are straight, abruptly relax them so that the hands fall limply. Try this with other muscles —tighten—then relax. Stretch, writhe, and wriggle yourself into a relaxed state.

For mental relaxation try consciously to think pleasant and restful thoughts, ignoring for a while the troubles of the day. Healthy forms of recreation (picnics, golf, etc.) are fine ways to release not only the physical tensions, but some of the mental ones as well.

WAKE UP REFRESHED

Exercise and the Heart

There are many misconceptions about exercise and its effect upon the heart. "Exercise is harmful." Nonsense. There is no evidence to support this contention. There is a large body of opinion which holds that exercise, appropriate to age and physical condition, continued through your life span will help to reduce the possibility of heart and blood vessel disease. Exercise, in mild form of course, is recommended as part of the recuperative phase in cases of heart or coronary disease. Evidence is also on hand that indicates exercise is beneficial to the function of the cardio-vascular system.

A healthy heart can obtain many benefits from a good conditioning program. Research has shown that the heart of a trained person has a smaller acceleration of pulse rate under stress, and that it returns more rapidly to its normal rate afterward than that of an untrained person; that it pumps more blood per beat at rest, and that it can pump more during exercise; that it has more richly developed small blood vessels supplying the heart muscle and that it functions more efficiently. An efficient cardio-vascular system means a better supply of blood and oxygen to the muscles (as blood is the carrier of these items) and a quicker recuperation after exertion, be it work, play, or exercise.

A CAUTIONARY NOTE. Persons over thirty-five years of age, and anyone who suspects she may have something wrong with her heart, should have a thorough medical examination before engaging in a vigorous exercise program. Experts have noted that a heart already injured by disease will suffer extra abuse through extreme forms of exercise. Sudden violent exertion after a period of inactivity is to be avoided.

EXERCISE YOUR HEART

Exercise, Strength, and Endurance

The strength and endurance of the body can be increased through regular exercise. Such improvements are primarily localized in the muscles and organs which are exercised——one cannot strengthen the arms and shoulders by exercising the legs. To improve the condition of all muscles one must undertake a program which will provide them all with work.

The strength of a muscle is measured by the amount of force that muscle can exert and is dependent upon the size and number of muscle fibres that can be brought into action at any one time and the frequency of the nerve impulses to them.

Endurance is concerned with the ability to repeat an action over and over again, or to sustain a muscular contraction.

Since the fuel for muscular contraction is carried in the blood, endurance is chiefly dependent upon the functioning of the cardio-respiratory system, (heart, blood vessels, and lungs)——that is, the ability of the body to transport food and oxygen to the muscles, and waste products away from them, efficiently.

The human body requires proper use to function efficiently and endure. The body is very different from a machine that wears out with use. Most persons have noted how the muscles of an arm or a leg in a cast become smaller and weaker the longer the arm or leg remains so encased. While this is a dramatic example it is in effect what happens to the muscles of the body in a milder way when these muscles are not used enough.

Exercise over and above the normal demands of daily living is essential to the development of an efficient, strong, and durable body. The resultant more pleasing appearance and sense of well-being are added benefits that cannot be overlooked.

LEAD A BALANCED LIFE

The
5BX
Plan
FOR MEN

---

5 Tested Exercises

11 Minutes a Day

The Official RCAF Fitness Plan

CAUTION

Before you start

If you have any doubt as to your capability to undertake this program, see your medical adviser.

You should not perform fast, vigorous, or highly competitive physical activity without gradually developing, and continuously maintaining, an adequate level of physical fitness, particularly if you are over the age of 30.

For whom

This exercise program has been designed for varying age groups covering male members of the Royal Canadian Air Force, Royal Canadian Air Cadets, and dependent children.

THE ROYAL CANADIAN AIR FORCE

The 5BX Plan

Here is a new scientifically designed approach to Physical Fitness which can develop an adequate level of reserve energy needed for vigorously positive well being and zestful living.

This plan enables you to get fit:

By yourself

At home

In your spare time

At your own rate of progress

Without discomfort and

in only 11 minutes a day.

5BX *means*
FIVE BASIC EXERCISES

The 5BX Plan is unique:

SIMPLE because it is easy to do, easy to follow.

PROGRESSIVE because you can develop your own personal fitness at your own rate, to your required level, without getting stiff or sore muscles.

BALANCED because you condition your muscles, your heart and lungs harmoniously for your daily needs.

COMPLETE because the principles of muscle and organic development are applied simultaneously and progressively.

SELF-MEASURING because it gives you clear cut "targets for fitness" for your age and body build, along with graduated standards for checking your progress.

CONVENIENT because you can do these exercises any place at your convenience, without gadgets,

Research Has Demonstrated that the 5BX Plan Will:

Increase the strength of the important muscle groups needed in everyday living.

Increase the ability of muscles used in essential body movements to function efficiently for long periods of time.

Increase the speed response of the important muscles of the body.

Keep the important muscles and joints of the body supple and flexible.

Improve the efficiency and capacity of the heart, lungs and other body organs.

Increase the capacity for physical exertion.

Why Should You Be So Concerned About Physical Fitness?

Mechanization, automation, and work-saving devices to make life easy are depriving us of desirable physical activity. Canadians, as a result, are in danger of deteriorating physically.

Here Are the Pertinent Facts

Muscles unless adequately exercised or used will become weak and inefficient. Let's take a look at some of the evidence which shows why regular vigorous exercise is so essential to physical well-being.

Weak back muscles are associated, in many cases, with lower back pain. It has been estimated that 90% of these backaches may be eliminated by increasing the strength of the back muscles through exercise.

A bulging, sagging abdomen resulting from weakened abdominal muscles is detrimental to good posture.

The efficiency and capacity of your heart, lungs and other organs can be improved by **regular vigorous** exercise.

A fit person is less susceptible to common injuries, and, if injured, recovers more rapidly.

The incidence of degenerative heart diseases may be greater in those who have not followed a physically active life.

Regular vigorous exercise plays an important role in controlling your weight.

Regular vigorous physical activity can help you to reduce emotional and nervous tension.

You are never too old to begin and follow a regular exercise program.

You Can Collect Valuable Dividends of Physical Efficiency from Your Daily Activities

Hidden in the simple activities we do every day are wonderful opportunities to get exercise and keep refreshed. Because we have developed an attitude of "doing it the easy way" we take short-cuts which seldom save time. Consequently we have developed habits to avoid physical exertion.

Here are some routine activities which can be turhed into small challenges that will help to maintain physical fitness once you have attained the suggested level of physical capacity for you. Make them a HABIT!!

Balance on one foot without support while putting on your socks or shoes.

Give yourself a vigorous rub-down with a rough towel after a shower.

Take the stairs two at a time instead of trudging up one at a time. Avoid elevators for short trips.

Lift your chair, don't shove it. Bend your knees fully and keep back straight when picking an object off the floor.

Welcome an opportunity to walk; look for ways you can walk a few blocks rather than ways in which to avoid walking. Step out smartly and breathe deeply.

PHYSICAL FITNESS

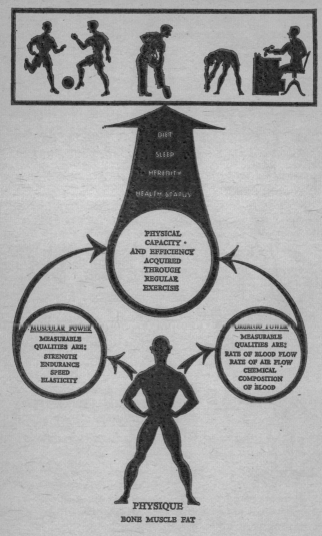

DIET

SLEEP

HEREDITY

HEALTH STATUS

PHYSICAL
CAPACITY
AND EFFICIENCY
ACQUIRED
THROUGH
REGULAR
EXERCISE

MUSCULAR POWER

MEASURABLE
QUALITIES ARE:
STRENGTH
ENDURANCE
SPEED
ELASTICITY

ORGANIC POWER

MEASURABLE
QUALITIES ARE:
RATE OF BLOOD FLOW
RATE OF AIR FLOW
CHEMICAL
COMPOSITION
OF BLOOD

PHYSIQUE
BONE MUSCLE FAT

Physical Fitness

The human body is made up mainly of bone, muscle and fat. Some 639 different muscles account for about 45% of the body weight. Each of these muscles has four distinct and measurable qualities which are of interest to us.

(1) It can produce force which can be measured as **strength** of muscle.

(2) It can store energy which permits it to work for extended periods of time independent of circulation. This is generally referred to as **muscular endurance.**

(3) It can shorten at varying rates. This is called **speed of contraction.**

(4) It can be stretched and will recoil. This is called the **elasticity** of muscle.

The combination of these four qualities of muscle is referred to as **MUSCULAR POWER.**

If muscles are to function efficiently, they must be continually supplied with energy fuel. This is accomplished by the blood which carries the energy fuel from lungs and digestive system to the muscles. The blood is forced through the blood vessels by the heart. The combined capacity to supply energy fuels to the working muscles is called **ORGANIC POWER.**

The capacity and efficiency with which your body can function depends on the degree of development of both your muscular and organic power through regular exercise. However, the level to which you can develop these powers is influenced by such factors as the type of body you inherit, the food you eat, presence or absence of disease, rest and sleep.

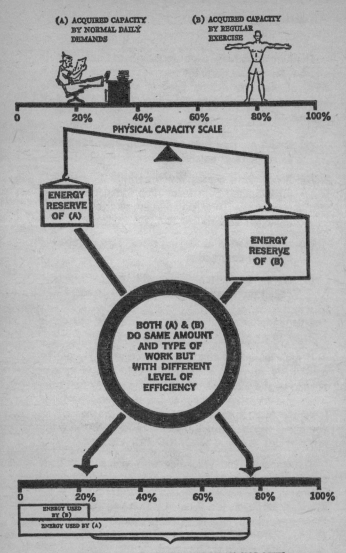

(A) ACQUIRED CAPACITY BY NORMAL DAILY DEMANDS

(B) ACQUIRED CAPACITY BY REGULAR EXERCISE

0   20%   40%   60%   80%   100%

PHYSICAL CAPACITY SCALE

ENERGY RESERVE OF (A)

ENERGY RESERVE OF (B)

BOTH (A) & (B) DO SAME AMOUNT AND TYPE OF WORK BUT WITH DIFFERENT LEVEL OF EFFICIENCY

0   20%   40%   60%   80%   100%

ENERGY USED BY (B)

ENERGY USED BY (A)

THIS IS THE AMOUNT OF ENERGY (B) HAS LEFT OVER TO ENJOY HIS RECREATIONAL ACTIVITIES

114

You are physically fit only when you have adequately developed your muscular and organic power to perform with the highest possible efficiency.

How Fit Should You Be?

Heredity and health determine the top limits to which your physical capacity can be developed. This is known as your potential physical capacity. This potential capacity varies from individual to individual. Most of us for example, could train for a lifetime and never come close to running a four minute mile simply because we weren't "built" for it.

The top level at which you can perform physically **right now** is called your "acquired capacity" because it has been acquired or developed through physical activity in your daily routines.

Your body, like a car, functions most efficiently well below its acquired capacity. A car, for example, driven at its top speed of, say, 110 miles per hour uses more gas per mile than when it is driven around 50-60 miles per hour, which is well below its capacity. Your body functions in the same way, in that the ratio of work performed to energy expended is better when it functions well below acquired capacity.

You can avoid wastage of energy by acquiring a level of physical capacity well above the level required to perform your normal daily tasks. This can be accomplished by supplementing your daily physical activity with a balanced exercise program performed regularly. Your capacity increases as you progressively increase the load on your muscular and organic systems.

Exercise will increase physical endurance and stamina thus providing a greater reserve of energy for leisure time activities.

The Contribution of Sports and Other Activities To Basic Physical Efficiency

Just as a balanced diet must be composed of a sufficient quantity of the proper kinds of foods to ensure that nutritional requirements are adequately met, so should a balanced physical activity program be composed of a sufficient quantity of the proper kind of physical activity so that all the important parts of the body are adequately exercised.

The parts of the body that require special attention are the muscles of the shoulder and arms, abdomen and back, legs, and the heart, lungs and blood vessels.

No single sport provides a truly balanced development for all parts of the body. This can only be acquired by regular participation in a number of carefully selected sports. Such participation, however, is not possible for the average person for a number of reasons—availability of play opportunity, time, finances. The most practical physical fitness scheme for most of us is participation in one or two sports supplemented by a balanced set of exercises. The 5BX program has been designed to bring physical fitness within the reach of any healthy person who is willing to devote 11 minutes a day to a simple but balanced set of exercises.

PHYSICAL EFFICIENCY COMPARISONS

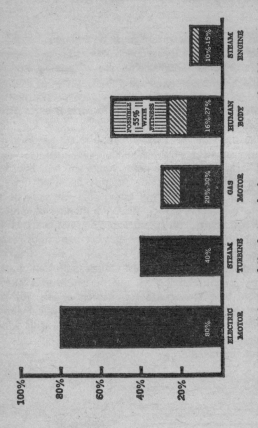

The efficiency of the human body compares poorly with the modern machine. However, through regular exercise its efficiency can be considerably increased.

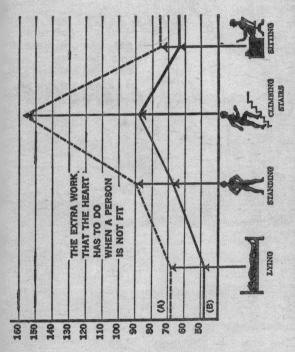

This graph illustrates the number of heart beats required for your different routine activities by a human being, (A) before and (B) after a regular vigorous exercise programme.

WALKING IS A "BEST" EXERCISE

Common Sense About Exercise

"It won't do you any good to exercise unless you do it until it hurts"—the saying goes. This is absolutely false. Although you may get some benefit from doing exercises until "it hurts", this is not necessary in order to acquire an adequate level of physical fitness. As a matter of fact, greater benefits can be derived from exercise by avoiding stiffness and soreness.

There are basically two ways in which you can avoid discomfort and still develop high levels of physical capacity:

Warm up properly before participating in any strenuous physical activity such as sprinting, handball, tennis, etc.

Start any training program at a low level of activity and work up by easy stages.

Warming Up

The 5BX Plan was designed so that no additional warmup is necessary in order to receive its maximum benefits.

The older one is, the more necessary proper warming up becomes to avoid "strained" muscles. The 5BX Plan has a built-in method of warmup. This is achieved in two ways:

—by the arrangement of the exercises; and

—by the manner in which these exercises are performed.

For example the first exercise is a stretching and loosening exercise which limbers up the large muscles of the body. In addition, this exercise should be started very slowly and easily, with a gradual increase in speed and vigor.

Let us see how this principle applies to exercise No. 1, which requires you to touch the floor. You should not force yourself to do it on the first attempt, but rather start by pushing down very gently and slowly as far as you can without undue strain—then on each succeeding try push down a little harder, and, at the same time, do the exercise a little faster so that by the end of two minutes you are touching the floor and moving at the necessary speed. All the exercises can be performed in this manner.

If you choose to do the exercises in the morning, and are a slow-starter, as soon as the alarm rings, stretch, arch your back, lift your legs, and start riding your bicycle.

Weight Control—Exercise

When you are overweight, you have more fat stored up in your body than is necessary or good for you.

You become overweight and flabby when you eat more "high-calorie food" than your body can use. Foods such as fats, sugars, starches, etc., supply the energy your body needs for its work. If you eat more high-calorie foods than is required for your daily work the surplus is stored in the form of fat. Fat is stored under the skin and around the internal organs.

Everyone has, or should have, some fat on his body. However excessive fat storage, particularly about vital organs, impairs physical efficiency and health. Fat makes the heart work harder since each extra pound of body fat requires about one quarter of a mile of blood vessels. It is obvious, therefore, that you cannot acquire the highest level of physical efficiency when you are overweight.

The accumulation of fat on your body can be prevented or reduced either by eating less high-calorie foods or increasing your physical activity. It is better still to combine these two by cutting down on high-calorie foods and increasing your physical activity by regular, frequent exercise.

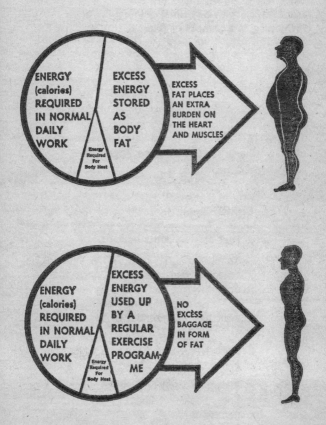

What Is It?

The 5BX Plan is composed of 6 charts arranged in progression. Each chart is composed of 5 exercises which are always performed in the same order and in the same maximum time limit, but, as you progress from chart to chart, there are slight changes in each basic exercise with a gradual demand for more effort.

Following is a sample of **Chart 3.**

NOTE: This chart is for illustration only. Charts for use start on Page 138.

CHART 3—

1 Feet astride, arms upward.

—Touch floor 6" outside left foot, again between feet and press once then 6" outside right foot, bend backward as far as possible, repeat, reverse direction after half the number of counts.

2 Back lying, feet 6" apart, arms clasped behind head.

—Sit up to vertical position, keep feet on floor, hook feet under chair, etc., only if necessary.

3 Front lying, hands interlocked behind the back.

—Lift head, shoulders, chest and both legs as high as possible.

—Keep legs straight, and raise chest and both thighs completely off floor.

4 Front lying, hands under the shoulders, palms flat on floor.

—Touch chin to floor in front of hands— touch forehead to floor behind hands before returning to up position.

—There are three definite movements, chin, forehead, arms straightened. DO NOT do in one continuous movement.

5 **Stationary run**—(Count a step each time left foot touches floor.) Lift feet approximately 4 inches off floor. After every 75 steps do 10 "half knee bends." Repeat this sequence until required number of steps is completed.

Half knee bends—Feet together, hands on hips, knees bent to form an angle of about 110 degrees. Do not bend knees past a right angle. Straighten to upright position, raising heel off floor, return to starting position each time.

Keep feet in contact with floor—the back upright and straight at all times.

The use of the rating scale is explained on pages 126–133.

A sample rating scale of Chart 3 is reproduced on the opposite page. Below is an explanation of Level.

These are the Physical Capacity levels, each indicated by a letter of the alphabet.

NOTE: This chart is for illustration only.
Charts for use start on Page 138.

PHYSICAL CAPACITY RATING SCALE

Level		EXERCISE				1 mile run	2 mile walk
	1	2	3	4	5	In minutes	
A+	30	32	47	24	550	8	25
A	30	31	45	22	540	8	25
A−	30	30	43	21	525	8	25
B+	28	28	41	20	510	8¼	26
B	28	27	39	19	500	8¼	26
B−	28	26	37	18	490	8¼	26
C+	26	25	35	17	480	8½	27
C	26	24	34	17	465	8½	27
C−	26	23	33	16	450	8½	27
D+	24	22	31	15	430	8¾	28
D	24	21	30	15	415	8¾	28
D−	24	20	29	15	400	8¾	29
Minutes for each exercise	2	1	1	1	6		

AGE GROUPS

12 YRS. MAINTAINS D+
13 YRS. MAINTAINS C+
14 YRS. MAINTAINS B+
35-39 YRS. MAINTAINS B
40-44 YRS. MAINTAINS C

FLYING CREW

AGE 40-44 MAINTAINS A+
AGE 45-49 MAINTAINS B

A sample rating scale of Chart 3 is reproduced on the opposite page. Below is an explanation of **Exercises.**

EXERCISES

Exercises 1, 2, 3 and 4 apply to the first four exercises described and illustrated on pages 124–125. The column headed 1 represents exercise 1 (toe touch), etc. The figures in each column indicate the number of times that each exercise is to be repeated in the time allotted for that exercise. Exercise 5 is running on the spot. Two activities may be substituted for it however, and if you prefer, you may run or walk the recommended distance in the required time in place of the stationary run of exercise 5.

NOTE: This chart is for illustration only. Charts for use start on Page 138.

PHYSICAL CAPACITY RATING SCALE

Level	EXERCISE					1 mile run	2 mile walk
	1	2	3	4	5	In minutes	
A+	30	32	47	24	550	8	25
A	30	31	45	22	540	8	25
A–	30	30	43	21	525	8	25
B+	28	28	41	20	510	8¼	26
B	28	27	39	19	500	8¼	26
B–	28.	26	37	18	490	8¼	26
C+	26	25	35	17	480	8½	27
C	25	24	34	17	465	8½	27
C–	26	23	33	16	450	8½	27
D+	24	22	31	15	430	8¾	28
D	24	21	30	15	415	8¾	28
D–	24	20	29	15	400	8¾	29
Minutes for each exercise	2	1	1	1	6		

AGE GROUPS
   12 YRS. MAINTAINS D+
   13 YRS. MAINTAINS C+
   14 YRS. MAINTAINS B+
   35-39 YRS. MAINTAINS B
   40-44 YRS. MAINTAINS C

FLYING CREW
   AGE 40-44 MAINTAINS A+
   AGE 45-49 MAINTAINS B

A sample rating scale of Chart 3 is reproduced on the opposite page. Below is an explanation of **Minutes for Each Exercise.**

A sample rating scale of Chart 3 is reproduced on the opposite page.

MINUTES FOR EACH EXERCISE

The allotted time for each exercise is noted here. These times remain the same throughout all the charts. Total time for exercises 1 through 5 is 11 minutes.

NOTE:

It is important that the exercises at any level be completed in 11 minutes. However, it is likely that in the early stages, an individual will complete certain exercises in less than the allotted time while others may require longer. In these circumstances the times allotted for individual exercises may be varied within the total 11 minute period.

130

PHYSICAL CAPACITY RATING SCALE

Level	EXERCISE					1 mile run	2 mile walk
	1	2	3	4	5	In minutes	
A+	30	32	47	24	550	8	25
A	30	31	45	22	540	8	25
A–	30	30	43	21	525	8	25
B+	28	28	41	20	510	8¼	26
B	28	27	39	19	500	8¼	26
B–	28	26	37	18	490	8¼	26
C+	26	25	35	17	480	8½	27
C	26	24	34	17	465	8½	27
C–	26	23	33	16	450	8½	27
D+	24	22	31	15	430	8¾	28
D	24	21	30	15	415	8¾	28
D–	24	20	29	15	400	8¾	29
Minutes for each exercise	2	1	1	1	6		

AGE GROUPS

12 YRS. MAINTAINS D+
13 YRS. MAINTAINS C+
14 YRS. MAINTAINS B+
35-39 YRS. MAINTAINS B
40-44 YRS. MAINTAINS C

FLYING CREW

AGE 40-44 MAINTAINS A+
AGE 45-49 MAINTAINS B

A sample rating scale of Chart 3 is reproduced on the opposite page. Below is an explanation of **How Far Should You Progress?**

HOW FAR SHOULD YOU PROGRESS?

The level of Physical Capacity to which you should progress is determined by your "Age Group."

Levels for "Flying Crew" are listed separately. See "Your Physical Capacity Level" on page 174.

PHYSICAL CAPACITY RATING SCALE

Level	1	2	3	4	5	1 mile run	2 mile walk
			EXERCISE			In minutes	
A+	30	32	47	24	550	8	25
A	30	31	45	22	540	8	25
A–	30	30	43	21	525	8	25
B+	28	28	41	20	510	8¼	26
B	28	27	39	19	500	8¼	26
B–	28	26	37	18	490	8¼	26
C+	26	25	35	17	480	8½	27
C	26	24	34	17	465	8½	27
C–	26	23	33	16	450	8½	27
D+	24	22	31	15	430	8¾	28
D	24	21	30	15	415	8¾	28
D–	24	20	29	15	400	8¾	29
Minutes for each exercise	2	1	1	1	6		

AGE GROUPS
12 YRS. MAINTAINS D+
13 YRS. MAINTAINS C+
14 YRS. MAINTAINS B+
35-39 YRS. MAINTAINS B
40-44 YRS. MAINTAINS C

FLYING CREW
AGE 40-44 MAINTAINS A+
AGE 45-49 MAINTAINS B

HOW TO BEGIN

Check your daily schedule and determine the time most convenient for you to do the exercises. It should be the same time each day.

Here are some suggested times:

—before breakfast;

—late morning or afternoon, at your place of employment;

—after your regular recreational period;

—in the evening just before you retire.

Regardless of the time you choose **START TODAY**.

Maximum Rate of Progression Through Chart 1 According to Age

20 years or under, at least 1 day at each level

20-29 years, at least 2 days at each level

30-39 years, at least 4 days at each level

40-49 years, at least 7 days at each level

50-59 years, at least 8 days each level

60 year and over, at least 10 days at each level

(If you feel stiff or sore, or if you are unduly breathless at any time, ease up and slow down your rate of progression. This is particularly applicable to the older age groups.)

A Note of Caution

Even if you feel able to start at a high level and progress at a faster rate than indicated—DON'T DO IT—Start at the bottom of Chart 1 and work up from level to level as recommended.

For best results from 5BX the exercises must be done **regularly.** Remember, it may take you 6, 8, 10 months or more of daily exercises to attain the level recommended for you, but once you have attained it, only 3 periods of exercise per week will maintain this level of physical capacity.

If for any reason (illness, etc.) you stop doing 5BX regularly and you wish to begin again, **do not** recommence at the level you had attained previously.

Do drop back several levels—until you find one you can do without undue strain. After a period of inactivity of longer than two months, or one month if caused by illness, it is recommended that you start again at Chart 1.

MAKE 5BX A HABIT

HOW to PROGRESS

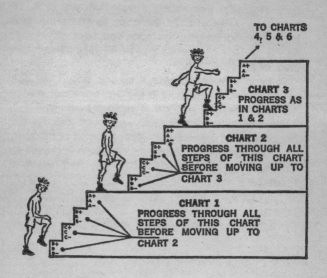

TO CHARTS
4, 5 & 6

CHART 3
PROGRESS AS
IN CHARTS
1 & 2

CHART 2
PROGRESS THROUGH ALL
STEPS OF THIS CHART
BEFORE MOVING UP TO
CHART 3

CHART 1
PROGRESS THROUGH ALL
STEPS OF THIS CHART
BEFORE MOVING UP TO
CHART 2

Start at the lowest Physical Capacity Level of Chart 1 (D–).

Repeat each exercise in the allotted time or do the 5 exercises in 11 minutes.

Move upward on the same chart to the next level (D) only after you can complete all the required movements at your present level within 11 minutes.

Continue to progress upward in this manner until you can complete all the required movements at level A+ within 11 minutes.

Now start at the bottom of Chart 2 (D–), and continue in this fashion upwards through the levels, and from chart to chart until you reach the level for your age group, i.e., age 35-39 (B Chart 3) does 32 levels from D– on Chart 1 to B on Chart 3.

CHART 1

PHYSICAL CAPACITY RATING SCALE

Level		EXERCISE				1/2 mile run	1 mile walk
	1	2	3	4	5	In minutes	
A+	20	18	22	13	400	5½	17
A	18	17	20	12	375	5½	17
A−	16	15	18	11	335	5½	17
B+	14	13	16	9	320	6	18
B	12	12	14	8	305	6	18
B−	10	11	12	7	280	6	18
C+	8	9	10	6	260	6½	19
C	7	8	9	5	235	6½	19
C−	6	7	8	4	205	6½	19
D+	4	5	6	3	175	7	20
D	3	4	5	3	145	7½	21
D−	2	3	4	2	100	8	21
Minutes for each exercise	2	1	1	1	6		

AGE GROUPS
6 YRS. MAINTAINS B
7 YRS. MAINTAINS A

Exercise 1

1 Feet astride, arms upward.

—Forward bend to floor touching then stretch upward and backward bend.

—Do not strain to keep knees straight.

2 Back lying, feet 6" apart, arms at sides.

—Sit up just far enough to see your heels.

—Keep legs straight, head and shoulders must clear the floor.

3 Front lying, palms placed under the thighs.

—Raise head and one leg, repeat using legs alternately.

—Keep leg straight at the knee, thighs must clear the palms.

(Count one each time second leg touches floor.)

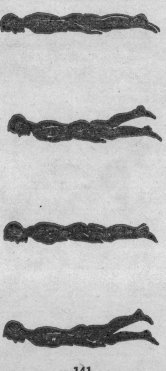

4 Front lying, hands under the shoulders, palms flat on the floor.

—Straighten arms lifting upper body, keeping the knees on the floor. Bend arms to lower body.

—Keep body straight from the knees, arms must be fully extended, chest must touch floor to complete one movement.

5 Stationary run—(Count a step each time left foot touches floor.) Lift feet approximately 4 inches off floor. Every 75 steps do 10 "scissor jumps." Repeat this sequence until required number of steps is completed.

Scissor jumps—Stand with right leg and left arm extended forward, and left leg and right arm extended backward.

Jump up—change position of arms and legs before landing. Repeat (arms shoulder high).

CHART 2

PHYSICAL CAPACITY RATING SCALE

Level	EXERCISE					1 mile run	2 mile walk
	1	2	3	4	5	In minutes	
A+	30	23	33	20	500	9	30
A	29	21	31	19	485	9	31
A−	28	20	29	18	470	9	32
B+	26	18	27	17	455	9½	33
B	24	17	25	16	445	9½	33
B−	22	16	23	15	440	9½	33
C+	20	15	21	14	425	10	34
C	19	14	19	13	410	10	34
C−	18	13	17	12	395	10	34
D+	16	12	15	11	380	10½	35
D	15	11	14	10	360	10½	35
D−	14	10	13	9	335	10½	35
Minutes for each exercise	2	1	1	1	6		

AGE GROUPS

8 YRS. MAINTAINS D−
9 YRS. MAINTAINS C−
10 YRS. MAINTAINS B−
11 YRS. MAINTAINS A−
45-49 YRS. MAINTAINS A+
50-60 YRS. MAINTAINS C+

Exercise 1

1 Feet astride, arms upward.

—Touch floor and press (bounce) once then stretch upward and backward bend.

Exercise 2

2 Back lying, feet 6" apart, arms at sides.

— "Sit up" to vertical position, keep feet on floor even if it is necessary to hook them under a chair.

Exercise 3

3 Front lying, palm placed under thighs.

—Raise head, shoulders, and both legs.

—Keep legs straight, both thighs must clear the palms.

4 Front lying, hands under the shoulder, palms flat on floor.

—Straighten arms to lift body with only palms and toes on the floor. Back straight.

—Chest must touch floor for each completed movement after arms have been fully extended.

5 Stationary run—(count a step each time left foot touches floor—Lift feet approximately 4 inches off floor). After every 75 steps, do 10 "astride jumps".

Repeat this sequence until required number of steps is completed.

Astride jumps—Feet together, arms at side.

Jump and land with feet astride and arms raised sideways to slightly above shoulder height. Return with a jump to the starting position for count of one.

Keep arms straight.

CHART 3

PHYSICAL CAPACITY RATING SCALE

Level	EXERCISE					1 mile run	2 mile walk
	1	2	3	4	5	In minutes	
A+	30	32	47	24	550	8	25
A	30	31	45	22	540	8	25
A−	30	30	43	21	525	8	25
B+	28	28	41	20	510	8¼	26
B	28	27	39	19	500	8¼	26
B−	28	26	37	18	490	8¼	26
C+	26	25	35	17	480	8½	27
C	26	24	34	17	465	8½	27
C−	26	23	33	16	450	8½	27
D+	24	22	31	15	430	8¾	28
D	24	21	30	15	415	8¾	28
D−	24	20	29	15	400	8¾	29
Minutes for each exercise	2	1	1	1	6		

AGE GROUPS
    12 YRS. MAINTAINS D+
    13 YRS. MAINTAINS C+
    14 YRS. MAINTAINS B+
35-39 YRS. MAINTAINS B
40-44 YRS. MAINTAINS C

FLYING CREW
    40-44 YRS. MAINTAINS A+
    45-49 YRS. MAINTAINS B

Exercise 1

1 Feet astride, arms upward.

—Touch floor 6" outside left foot, again between feet and press once then 6" outside right foot, bend backward, as far as possible, repeat, reverse direction after half the number of counts.

2 Back lying, feet 6″ apart, arms clasped behind head.

—Sit up to vertical position, keep feet on floor, hook feet under chair, etc., only if necessary.

Exercise 3

3 Front lying, hands interlocked behind the back.

—Lift head, shoulders, chest and both legs as high as possible.

—Keep legs straight, and raise chest and both thighs completely off floor.

4 Front lying, hands under the shoulders, palms flat on floor.

—Touch chin to floor in front of hands—touch forehead to floor behind hands before returning to up position.

—There are three definite movements, chin, forehead, arms straightened. DO NOT do in one continuous movement.

5 Stationary run—(Count a step each time left foot touches floor.) Lift feet approximately 4 inches off floor. After every 75 steps do 10 "half knee bends."

Repeat this sequence until required number of steps is completed.

Half knee bends—Feet together, hands on hips, knees bent to form an angle of about 110 degrees. Do not bend knees past a right angle.

Straighten to upright postion, raising heel off floor, return to starting position each time.

Keep feet in contact with floor—the back upright and straight at all times.

CHART 4

PHYSICAL CAPACITY RATING SCALE

Level	EXERCISE					1 mile run	2 mile walk
	1	2	3	4	5	In minutes	
A+	30	22	50	42	400	7	19
A	30	22	49	40	395	7	19
A–	30	22	49	37	390	7	19
B+	28	21	47	34	380	7¼	20
B	28	21	46	32	375	7¼	20
B–	28	21	46	30	365	7¼	20
C+	26	19	44	28	355	7½	21
C	26	19	43	26	345	7½	21
C–	26	19	43	24	335	7½	21
D+	24	18	41	21	325	7¾	23
D	24	18	40	19	315	7¾	23
D–	24	18	40	17	300	7¾	23
Minutes for each exercise	2	1	1	1	6		

AGE GROUPS
    15 YRS. MAINTAINS D–
16-17 YRS. MAINTAINS C+
25-29 YRS. MAINTAINS A+
30-34 YRS. MAINTAINS C–

FLYING CREW
    30-34 YRS. MAINTAINS B
    35-39 YRS. MAINTAINS C–

Exercise 1

1 Feet astride, arms upward.

—Touch floor outside left foot, between feet, press once then outside right foot, circle bend backwards as far as possible, reverse directions after half the number of counts.

—Keep arms above head and make full circle, bending backward past vertical each time.

2 Back lying, legs straight, feet together, arms straight overhead.

—Sit up and touch the toes keeping the arms and legs straight. Use chair to hook feet under only if necessary.

—Keep arms in contact with the sides of the head throughout the movement.

3 Front lying, hands and arms stretched sideways.

—Lift head, shoulders, arms, chest and both legs as high as possible.

—Keep legs straight, raise chest and both thighs completely off floor.

Exercise 4

4 Front lying, palms of hands flat on floor, approximately 1 foot from ears directly to side of head.

—Straighten arms to lift body.

—Chest must touch floor for each completed movement.

5 Stationary run—(Count a step each time left foot touches floor.) Lift knees waist high.

Every 75 steps do 10 "semi-squat jumps."

Repeat this sequence until required number of steps is completed.

Semi-squat jumps—Drop to a half crouch position with hands on knees and arms straight, keep back as straight as possible, right foot slightly ahead of left.

—Jump to upright position with body straight and feet leaving floor. Reverse position of feet before landing. Return to half crouch position and repeat.

CHART 5

PHYSICAL CAPACITY RATING SCALE

Level	EXERCISE					1 mile run
	1	2	3	4	5	Mins : Secs
A+	30	40	50	44	500	6 : 00
A	30	39	49	43	485	6 : 06
A–	30	38	48	42	475	6 : 09
B+	28	36	47	40	465	6 : 12
B	28	35	46	39	455	6 : 15
B–	28	34	45	38	445	6 : 21
C+	26	32	44	36	435	6 : 27
C	26	31	43	35	420	6 : 33
C–	26	30	42	34	410	6 : 39
D+	24	28	41	32	400	6 : 45
D	24	27	40	31	385	6 : 51
D–	24	26	39	30	375	7 : 00
Minutes for each exercise	2	1	1	1	6	

AGE GROUP
18-25 YRS. MAINTAINS C

FLYING CREW
UNDER 25 YRS. MAINTAINS B+
25-29 YRS. MAINTAINS D+

Exercise 1

1 Feet astride, arms upward, hands clasped, arms straight.

— Touch floor outside left foot, between feet, press once then outside right foot, circle bend backwards as far as possible.

Reverse direction after half the number of counts.

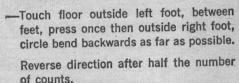

Exercise 2

2 Back lying, legs straight, feet together, hands clasped behind head.

—Sit up and raise legs in bent position at same time twist to touch right elbow to left knee. This completes one movement.

Alternate the direction of twist each time.

—Keep feet off floor when elbow touches knee.

Exercise 3

3 Front lying, arms extended overhead.

—Raise arms, head, chest and both legs as high as possible.

—Keep legs and arms straight, chest and both thighs completely off floor.

4 Front lying, hands under shoulder, palms flat on floor.

—Push off floor and clap hands before returning to starting position.

—Keep body straight during the entire movement. Hand clap must be heard.

5 **Stationary run**—(Count a step each time left foot touches floor. Lift knees waist high.)

Every 75 steps do 10 "semi-spread eagle jumps."

Repeat this sequence until required number of steps is completed.

Semi-spread eagle jumps—Feet together, drop to a half crouch position hands on knees with arms straight.

—Jump up to feet astride swing arms overhead in mid-air, return directly to starting position on landing.

—Raise hands above head level, spread feet at least shoulder width apart in astride position before landing with feet together.

CHART 6

PHYSICAL CAPACITY RATING SCALE

Level	EXERCISE					1 mile run
	1	2	3	4	5	Mins : Secs
A+	30	50	40	40	600	5 : 00
A	30	48	39	39	580	5 : 03
A–	30	47	38	38	555	5 : 09
B+	28	45	37	36	530	5 : 12
B	28	44	36	35	525	5 : 18
B–	28	43	35	34	515	5 : 24
C+	26	41	34	32	505	5 : 27
C	26	40	33	31	495	5 : 33
C–	26	39	32	30	485	5 : 39
D+	24	37	31	28	475	5 : 45
D	24	36	30	27	460	5 : 51
D–	24	35	29	26	450	6 : 00
Minutes for each exercise	2	1	1	1	6	

PHYSICAL CAPACITIES IN THIS CHART ARE USUALLY FOUND ONLY IN CHAMPION ATHLETES.

Exercise 1

1 Feet astride, arms upward, hands reverse clasped, arms straight.

—Touch floor outside left foot, between feet, press once then outside right foot, circle bend backwards as far as possible.

Reverse direction after half the number of counts.

—Keep hands tightly reverse clasped at all times.

2 Back lying, legs straight, feet together, arms straight over the head.

—Sit up and at the same time lifting both legs to touch the toes in a pike (V) position.

—Keep feet together, legs and arms straight, all of the upper back and legs clear floor, fingers touch toes each time.

3 Front lying, arms extended over head.

—Raise arms, head, chest and both legs as high as possible then press back once.

—Keep legs and arms straight—chest and both thighs completely off floor.

4 Front lying, hands under shoulders, palms flat on floor.

—Push off floor and slap chest before returning to starting position.

—Keep body straight during the entire movement, chest slap must be heard.

5 Stationary run—(count a step each time left foot touches floor—lift knees waist high).

Every 75 steps do 10 "jack jumps".

Repeat this until required number of steps is completed.

Jack jumps—Feet together, knees bent, sit on heels, finger tips touch floor.

—Jump up, raise legs waist high, keep legs straight and touch toes in midair.

—Keep legs straight, raise feet level to "standing waist height". Touch toes each time.

Your Physical Capacity Level

Each age group is given a Physical Capacity level to attain; that is, a goal which they should try to reach.

The Physical Capacity levels in this plan are based on the expectation of average individuals.

With every average, there are individuals who surpass it, and those who fall below it. In terms of the 5BX Plan and the goals, this means that there will be some men who are capable of progressing beyond the level indicated, and on the other hand, there will be persons who will never attain this average level.

If you feel able to move further through the charts than your Physical Capacity level, by all means do so. If, on the contrary, you experience great difficulty in approaching this level, you should stop at a level which you feel to be within your capability. It is impossible to predict accurately a level for each individual who uses this program. Use the goals as guides, and apply them with common sense.

Here Are a Few Tips:

When you start, defeat the first desire to skip a day; then defeat all such desires as they occur. This exercise program has plenty of bite; the longer you do it the more you will enjoy it.

As you progress well into the program you may find certain levels almost impossible to complete in 11 minutes—work hard at that level—it may take some days or even weeks—then suddenly you will find yourself sailing ahead again.

Counting the steps in exercise 5 can be difficult. You can lose count very easily at times. If you have this problem, here is an easy way to overcome it. Divide the total number of steps required by 75 and note the answer—place a row of buttons, corresponding in number to this answer, on a handy table or chair. Now count off your first 75 steps—do your ten required movements—and move the first button. Repeat until all the buttons have been removed, finishing up with any left over steps.

For diversity, occasionally an exercise from the previous chart may be substituted.